The Oscars

VICKY SHIPTON

Level 3

Series Editors: Andy Hopkins and Jocelyn Potter

Pearson Education Limited
Edinburgh Gate, Harlow,
Essex CM20 2JE, England
and Associated Companies throughout the world.

ISBN 978-0-582-45334-0

First published 2001
Fifth impression 2007

Copyright © Vicky Shipton 2001
Cover design by Ten Toes Design
Illustration p.37 by George Hollingworth

Design by John Fordham
Colour reproduction by Spectrum Colour
Printed in China
SWTC/05

Published by Pearson Education Limited in association with Penguin
Books Ltd, both companies being subsi diaries of Pearson Plc

Photograph acknowledgements:
Ronald Grant: pp.2 and 25; Kobal: pp.4, 7, 12,
13, 17, 20, 23, 25 (courtesy of 20ᵗʰ Century Fox),
27, 29, 31, 33 and 38.

For a complete list of titles available in the Penguin Readers series, please write to your local
Pearson Education office or to: Penguin Readers Marketing Department,
Pearson Education, Edinburgh Gate, Harlow, Essex CM20 2JE.

Contents

Introduction

Why are the Oscars so important? For many movie-makers, an Oscar is a sign that they are making great art. After they have won an Oscar, actors and actresses are usually offered lots of work. They can earn more for each movie, too!

★　★　★

How did a little man called Oscar become so important in Hollywood? Why do most actors and actresses love him? Why do some hate him? Why does the world watch the movie awards show?

An Oscar can make a movie a big success. It can make an actor a star immediately. Most movie-makers think that Oscar night is Hollywood's finest hour.

This book shows why Oscar is the big man in Hollywood. It also looks *behind* the smiles and speeches of the awards. What is the real story of Oscar night?

★　★　★

Vicky Shipton is from Michigan, in the United States. She lived in Turkey and England for a long time. When she went back to the US, she lived in Chicago for four years. Now she lives in Madison, Wisconsin, with her husband and two daughters. During the cold winters in Wisconsin, she loves to watch movies.

Can you win an Oscar?

How much do you know about movies and the Oscars?
Answer these questions and see.

1. Who was the youngest actor to win an Oscar for her acting?
   a) Tatum O'Neal   b) Judy Garland   c) Liza Minelli

2. Who never goes to the Oscars?
   a) Jane Fonda   b) Woody Allen   c) Steven Spielberg

3. Which actor has won the most Oscars?
   a) Tom Hanks   b) Katherine Hepburn   c) Jack Nicholson

4. What movie won a Best Director Oscar for Steven Spielberg?
   a) *Jaws*   b) *Raiders of the Lost Ark*   c) *Schindler's List*

5. Which actor has received more nominations than any other actor?
   a) Tom Hanks   b) Jack Nicholson   c) Robert Redford

6. What does the presenter of an Oscar receive?
   a) a photo   b) a little Oscar   c) almost $10,000 in gifts

7. Which movies win most Oscars?
   a) serious movies   b) funny movies   c) scary movies

8. Which movie didn't win an Oscar for Best Picture?
   a) *Dances with Wolves*   b) *Psycho*   c) *American Beauty*

Did you win an Oscar? Look on page 41.

Everybody loves Oscar!

One of the most important men in Hollywood is just thirty-four centimeters tall! He weighs less than four kilograms! His name? Oscar, of course. "Oscar" is the popular name for the most famous award in the movie business.

★ **What's in a name?** ★
How did this little gold man get his name? There are many different stories. Some people think that the name was given by a movie historian in 1931. When she saw the award, she said, "It looks like my Uncle Oscar!"

★ ★ ★ ★ ★ ★

Why are the Oscars so important? For many movie-makers, an Oscar is a sign that they are making great art. After they have won an Oscar, actors and actresses are usually offered lots of work. They can earn more for each movie, too!

For movie studios also, success at the Oscars means big money. People all around the world are watching Hollywood on Oscar night. After a movie has won an Oscar for Best Picture, it is immediately back in movie theaters.

In the beginning . . .

Money was also important to the beginning of the Oscars. In the 1920s, the movie business was not very old, but it was already very successful. But not everybody in Hollywood was happy. Movie workers wanted more money. Movie studios wanted to pay less money. The problem was growing. In 1927, a group of Hollywood workers started an academy (the AMPAS). Actors, directors, producers, and studios were in the organization. It helped the studios and their workers agree about money.

There was another reason for the start of the Academy. The business had enemies at the time. Some politicians and church groups thought that movies were bad for people. The new academy tried to answer these enemies. They made a list of all the good movies that were made between August 1, 1927 and July 31, 1928. This was the start of the awards. The Academy chose the nominations but five judges decided the winners.

They gave 12 awards:
2 for actors
3 for writers
3 for directors
1 for producers
3 for movies

The first winners of Best Actor and Actress awards are not very famous today—Emil Jannings was the Best Actor and Janet Gaynor was the Best Actress. The Academy gave two Best Picture awards. Both of the movies were silent, but a special award was also given to the first movie with sound, *The Jazz Singer*. The Academy gave a special award to funny man Charlie Chaplin, too.

The Academy had a dinner party where they gave the awards to the winners. The dinner cost ten dollars and only 150 people were invited. There were no surprises that night. Everybody knew the winners three months before the party. Best Actress Janet Gaynor said later, "I still remember that night as very special." But the best part for her was meeting Douglas Fairbanks, a famous movie star at the time.

After 1933, the Academy did not help Hollywood workers and studios in their discussions about money, but they continued to give awards. The awards did not change much for fifteen years, but

Charlie Chaplin

they became more and more popular. In 1933, the Academy president was director Frank Capra. He called the awards the "world's number one" news story of the year.

Oscar grows up

The Oscars show has always been in Los Angeles. In 1952, it was in Los Angeles and New York at the same time. The Academy did that for only five years.

The show has moved from theater to theater in LA. As it gets bigger, a bigger theater is needed. Now the Academy is building a big shopping center in Hollywood. It will have stores, movie theaters, and a big theater for the Oscars show. It will cost over sixty-seven million dollars. The Oscars will finally have a home.

★ **Smile, please!** ★

At first, the Academy did not want to sell the name of the theater. Then the Kodak company offered seventy-five million dollars. Now it is called the Kodak Theater . . . but only for twenty years.

★ ★ ★ ★ ★ ★ ★ ★ ★

Of course, television is very important to the Oscars' success. At first, the movie business thought that television was the enemy. People at home in front of the television were not out in movie theaters!

But many movie-makers changed their minds after the Oscars were on television for the first time in 1952. Interest in the awards grew and grew. Now over 100 million people around the world watch the awards. Many see the show as it happens. Others see it a day or two later on video. It is one of the most popular television programs in the world.

The big awards

Today the most important Oscars are for:
>**Best Picture ***
>**Best Actor**
>**Best Actress**
>**Best Supporting Actor**
>**Best Supporting Actress**
>**Best Director**

But what is a "Supporting" Actor or Actress? Sometimes it is not easy to decide. Is someone the main actor in a movie, or just a supporting actor? The actors and the studios decide this. Some people think that the awards for Best Supporting Actor or Actress are easier to win.

OSCAR MEMORIES ★ ★ ★ ★ ★ ★ ★ ★ ★ ★ ★

- Comedy star Robin Williams had a serious part in *Good Will Hunting*. When the studio talked about an Oscar, Williams did not try for Best Actor. He chose to try for Best Supporting Actor . . . and he won!
- In 1999, British actress Judy Dench won a Best Supporting Actress award for *Shakespeare in Love*. She played Queen Elizabeth I. At the awards, she joked that she was only in the movie for a few minutes!
- Anthony Hopkins won a Best Actor Oscar for *The Silence of the Lambs* in 1992. In the movie, he played the dangerous killer, Hannibal Lecter. The actor was not in the movie for very long—less time than any other Best Actor winner has been in

---

* picture: another word for movie.

People loved to hate Hannibal Lecter.

a movie. But everyone agreed that Hopkins was great.

- In 1983, Linda Hunt won a Best Supporting Actress Oscar for her work in *The Year of Living Dangerously.* She was in the movie with Mel Gibson. The movie was about Indonesia. She played a photographer . . . and a man. No other woman has won an Oscar for playing a man.

★ ★ ★ ★ ★ ★ ★ ★ ★ ★ ★ ★ ★ ★ ★ ★ ★ ★

The voting

How are the winners chosen? The members of the Academy vote for them. There are over 5,000 members. They all work in the movie business.

Actors and actresses **1375**

Producers **450**

Writers **416**

Directors **351**

Others **2633**

Members of the Academy (AMPAS)

Members of the Academy need to see as many movies as possible during the year. Members in Los Angeles can go to the Academy's theater.

Step 1:
In January, Academy members suggest nominations for the Oscars. Everybody can make a suggestion for Best Picture. For the other Oscars, a member only makes nominations for people who do his or her job in the movie business. So only actors and actresses can make nominations for acting awards.

Step 2:
The Academy counts all the suggestions. In February, it gives a list of five nominations for each Oscar. This is given very early in the morning—around 8:00 A.M. in New York.

That is five o'clock in the morning in Los Angeles! This is because the Academy wants the lists to be on the early morning news shows in the US.

Next, the Academy starts to show the movies to members in Los Angeles, New York, and London. There is not much time, and some members of the Academy do not see all of the movies. But this does not always stop them voting!

★ **A new life** ★

Life changes quickly for actors and actresses who are nominated. They are suddenly more popular than ever. The telephone never stops ringing. Some give as many TV and magazine interviews as possible. They think that maybe this will help them to win. Some actors even start working in theater. They think that this can also help them to win.

★   ★   ★   ★   ★   ★   ★   ★   ★

Step 3:

In March, the members of the Academy make the final vote. This time, they choose the winners. But before the big night, only three people in the Academy know who the winners are.

Step 4:

Two weeks before the Oscars, the Academy has an Oscar lunch. Everyone with a nomination can go. At the lunch they are asked to think about their speeches!

Step 5:

Near the end of March, it is Oscar night at last. Finally, everybody learns who has won.

With a little help . . .

Of course, movie studios want their movies to win. They work hard during the voting. This can be very expensive. Big studios sometimes spend between 0.5 and 1.5 million dollars to help their movies with Academy voters.

How can they do this? First, they send videos of the movie to members. When the studio sent *Titanic* to voters, there was a note from director James Cameron with the video. In the letter, Cameron asked voters to "please, please" see the movie in a theater, if possible.

In the past, movie studios could give gifts to voters. *My Left Foot* was a movie about the life of Christie Brown. Brown could not walk. He wrote and painted with his left foot. The studios wanted the movie to win Best Picture. They showed it in a theater in Washington, DC, and on every chair there was a candy in the shape of a foot. (But people in wheelchairs did not get the candy!)

The movie *Donny Brasco* was a true story about criminals in New York. The movie studio sent voters a little box. When the box was opened, a New York voice said, "fuggedaboudit" ("Forget about it"). This was a line from the movie.

Of course the gifts became more and more expensive, and finally the Academy stopped them. Now movie studios can only send the movie and the music to voters.

Oscar day

At last, the big day arrives. If you are nominated, what goes through your mind?

March 24

Woke up at 9 A.M. It's Oscar Day! After breakfast, I sit by the hotel pool. The sky is blue and the sun is hot, but I don't really have a good time. I'm worrying about tonight!

11.00 A.M. People arrive to help. First my face, then my hair. Finally, my clothes. Calvin Klein or Versace? (Life is hard!!)

2:30 P.M. I leave for the show with my driver. We sit in traffic for two hours! I hate the traffic in LA!

4.30 P.M. At last, I arrive at the red carpet. There are photographers everywhere. I see last year's Best Actor. He doesn't know me.

5:00 P.M. We get our seats in the theater. There are famous faces all around me.

6:00 P.M. Matt Damon is the presenter for Best Supporting Actress. I can see five faces on the big television. One of them is mine! Matt opens the envelope and reads my name. I've won! I can't remember my speech. I try to thank everybody, but I forget a lot of names. I'm so nervous!

8:00 P.M. Behind the stage, I talk to reporters and television people from around the world. I still can't believe this! It's like a dream.

8:30 P.M. I go to the first party of the night. Last year's Best Actor is there—now he knows me!

4:30 A.M. I'm on the morning TV news. More questions.

5:30 A.M. Bed!

6:30 A.M. The telephone rings. A friend in New York is shouting, "Well done!"

"Good evening, everybody"

You need a special person to introduce one of the biggest shows in the world. The host is one of the most important people at the Oscars.

One of the most popular hosts is probably Billy Crystal. He has hosted the show six times. One year, he rode onto the stage on a horse. (He was in a cowboy movie that year!)

Billy Crystal always gets a lot of laughs.

There have been a lot of famous hosts for the Oscars:

- Bob Hope hosted the show eighteen times between 1939 and 1977.
- Actor Jack Lemmon has hosted it four times.
- TV-star Johnny Carson hosted the show five times. He was the presenter of a late night "talk show" on American television. After the 1979 awards, Carson said, "The show had two good hours." But the show was four hours!
- Another late night TV presenter, David Letterman, hosted the show in 1995. He asked Tom Hanks to come onto the stage. The actor had to help with a dog trick! A lot of people did not like Letterman as the host. Some thought

that he was not serious enough about the awards. Letterman has said that he will never be the host again!

- In 1972, there were five hosts—Charlton Heston, Carol Burnett, Clint Eastwood, Michael Caine, and Rock Hudson. On the way to the show, Charlton Heston had car trouble. He was late. Clint Eastwood had to read some of Heston's lines. Not all of them made sense when they were read by a different actor.

- Actress Whoopi Goldberg was the host in 1999. One of the year's movies was *Elizabeth*, about Queen Elizabeth I. At the start of the show, Whoopi came onto the stage in queen's clothes. She changed her clothes eleven times during the show. Her clothes were always from one of the year's movies.

Whoopi Goldberg

AN OSCAR MEMORY ★ ★ ★ ★ ★ ★ ★ ★ ★ ★

Usually, the show is too long. But one year it was short by twenty minutes. The host, Jerry Lewis, asked the band to play. Some movie stars danced on stage!

★ ★ ★ ★ ★ ★ ★ ★ ★ ★ ★ ★ ★ ★ ★ ★ ★ ★

The person with the envelope

Some actors and actresses will never win an Oscar, but they want to be part of the Oscar show. Maybe this is why many of them want to present an award.

Usually, bigger stars present the more important awards. Often, the presenters are last year's winners. Some stars are not very happy if the Academy asks them to present a "small" Oscar for technical work! In fact, a lot of these technical Oscars are presented in a different show. The Academy usually shows a quick video of these winners during the "big" show.

The presenter reads out the names of the nominated actors, movies, or directors. Then he or she opens the envelope and tells everybody the winner.

- The most important award is the one for Best Picture. Only a few people have presented this award more than once:
  Twice: Gary Cooper, Warren Beatty, Sidney Poitier, and Al Pacino.
  Three times: Elizabeth Taylor
  Four times: Audrey Hepburn
  Five times: Jack Nicholson

- John Wayne presented the Best Picture award in 1978. Everyone knew that America's most famous movie cowboy was sick. They stood and clapped for a long time. Wayne died three months later.

★

- Actor Christopher Reeve presented an award in 1996. After an accident on a horse, the actor could not move any part of his body. When he came onto the stage, the crowd stood and clapped for over a minute. Reeve talked about the need for movies with good messages. After his speech, the crowd stood again and clapped.

★

- One person gave himself an Oscar—Walt Disney!

★

- A man took off all his clothes and ran across the stage. The presenter that year was David Niven. The British actor was famous for his quick jokes. He pointed to the man and said, "This is the only laugh he will ever get."

Every year after the show, the presenters are given a gift box. It usually has expensive wine and candy in it. Sometimes there is a watch. Companies give these because they want the stars to have them. The gift box can cost almost $10,000.

AN OSCAR MEMORY ★ ★ ★ ★ ★ ★ ★ ★ ★ ★

One year, actress Sharon Stone was presenting an Oscar. She realized that she did not have the envelope. She told the crowd to close their eyes and think very hard about the winner. The crowd loved it.

★ ★ ★ ★ ★ ★ ★ ★ ★ ★ ★ ★ ★ ★ ★ ★ ★ ★ ★

And the winner is . . :

Every year, a new list of Oscar winners goes into the history books.

Who is the most successful actress?
One actress has been more successful than every other woman at the Oscars. Katharine Hepburn has won four times. Her first Academy Award was in 1933. Her last Oscar, for Best Actress in *On Golden Pond*, was almost fifty years later! With twelve nominations, she is also the actress who has been nominated the most times.

Who is the most successful actor?
- Jack Nicholson has been nominated more than every other actor—twelve times! He has won three Oscars. Two were for Best Actor and one was for Best Supporting Actor.
- Spencer Tracy, Gary Cooper, Marlon Brando, Fredric March, and Tom Hanks have also each won two Oscars.
- Tom Hanks had two very good years. He won in 1994 for *Philadelphia* and then in 1995 for *Forrest Gump*.

Who are the oldest and youngest winners?
- Jessica Tandy is the oldest Oscar winner. She won an Oscar for Best Actress at the age of eighty-two for *Driving Miss Daisy*.
- The youngest Oscar winner was Shirley Temple. She won a special Oscar in 1935, when she was just five! The youngest person to win an Oscar for her acting was Tatum O'Neal in 1974. She was nine when she acted in *Paper Moon* with her father, Ryan O'Neal.

Forrest Gump said, "Life is like a box of chocolates."

Who has won the most Oscars?
The answer is Walt Disney. He won twenty-six Academy Awards. He also won the most Oscars in one year. In 1953, Disney received four awards!

Who has received the most nominations?
The people with the most nominations were not actors or directors. Cedric Gibbons was nominated forty times for his

art work. Edith Head was nominated thirty-three times for clothes design. She was nominated every year for nineteen years. She won eight Oscars.

What happens when the Academy voters cannot decide?

It does not happen very often, but sometimes the number of votes for two people or movies are exactly the same. When this happens, the Academy gives two awards.

- In 1932, Wallace Berry from *The Champ* and Fredric March from *Dr. Jekyll and Mr. Hyde* were both given the award for Best Actor.
- In 1969, Katharine Hepburn won the Best Actress award for *The Lion in Winter* and Barbra Streisand won for *Funny Girl*.

Which winner's parents also won Oscars?

In 1973, Liza Minnelli won a Best Actress Oscar for *Cabaret*. Her mom, Judy Garland, won a special Oscar in 1939. Her dad, Vincente Minnelli, won a Best Director Oscar in 1958.

★ **Double success** ★

These actors all played the same person in two different movies. Each actor was nominated both times.
- Bing Crosby in *Going My Way* and *The Bells of Saint Mary's*.
- Paul Newman in *The Hustler* and *The Color of Money*.
- Al Pacino in *The Godfather I* and *The Godfather II*.

★　★　★　★　★　★　★　★　★

"You like me!"

Of course, when they win an Oscar, actors and actresses have to give a speech. Louise Fletcher won the Best Actress Oscar for *One Flew Over the Cuckoo's Nest*. In the movie, she played a bad nurse. When she won she said, "I've loved being hated by you."

Some actors and actresses seem lost without a writer's lines. Some winners are just too excited when they give their speeches:
- In 1991, director Jonathan Demme said "uh" or "um" ninety times in his speech.
- When Sally Field won an Oscar for Best Actress in *Places in the Heart*, she shouted, "You like me, you really like me!" It was true, but not so many liked her speech!

One problem with the Oscar show has been long speeches. Winners sometimes want to thank everybody. In 1943, one winner's speech was very long. After the show, she thought that she spoke for about five minutes. Other people knew that her speech was over one hour!

Now the Academy asks winners to give short speeches. When someone speaks for too long, the band begins to play music. Everybody knows what this means: "Leave the stage." But not every winner has listened to this message. When Cuba Gooding, Jr.* won a Best Supporting Actor Oscar for *Jerry McGuire*, the music started during his speech. Gooding did not stop. He just shouted louder!

---

*Jr.: short for "Junior." It means that a man has the same name as his father.

"It doesn't mean anything!"

In 1978, Woody Allen's movie *Annie Hall* had five nominations. He decided not to go to the Oscars in Los Angeles. He stayed in New York and played in a band in a restaurant, as usual. Even after *Annie Hall* won, Woody still was not interested. In an interview he said, "The Oscar didn't mean anything to me." Woody Allen has had other nominations, but he has not changed his mind. He still does not go to the Oscars. He even goes to bed without knowing the winners. In his opinion, the Academy voters "don't know what they're doing."

Woody Allen is not interested in the Oscars.

Not many actors and directors have the same opinion, but Woody Allen is not alone. In 1971, George C. Scott won the Oscar for Best Actor in *Patton*. He refused the award. In his opinion, his movies were too serious for a silly awards show. Spanish director Luis Buñuel was not happy when he was given an Oscar. He did not want one in his home!

Other actors have questioned the idea of the Oscars. Meryl Streep once compared movies with paintings: "This blue is better than that blue?" It was crazy "to have winners and losers in art." But, Streep has won two Oscars. She accepted both of them.

Some stars have changed their minds after they won an Oscar:

John Wayne
Before the Oscar: "You can't drink or eat an award."
After the Oscar: "The Oscar is a beautiful thing to have."

Dustin Hoffman
Before the Oscar: In his opinion, movie awards were silly.
After the Oscar: "I am proud."

Jane Fonda
Before the Oscar: She was not interested in the award.
After the Oscar: In her speech she said, "There's a lot I could say tonight. But this isn't the time or place. So I'll just say 'Thank you.'"

It's not about winning

Some actors and actresses have come to the Oscars with a different idea. With the eyes of the world on them, they want to send a message about something important to them.

In 1973, Marlon Brando did not come for his Best Actor award. He sent American Indian Sacheen Littlefeather. She refused the award. She talked about how badly the United States government acted toward American Indians. Littlefeather was very scared during her speech. Brando never received this Oscar, but he took all of his other Oscars!

After she won in 1978, Vanessa Redgrave did not say much about movies. She used her speech to give her opinions about problems between Palestine and Israel. A lot of people at the awards were angry about this. The next winner spoke about it in his speech. He was "sick and tired" of speeches like Redgrave's, he said.

In the same year, there were two movies about the Vietnam War. Some people did not like the way movies showed the war. There was trouble outside the theater. But that year, Jane Fonda won the Best Actress Oscar for *Coming Home*, one of the movies about Vietnam. She wanted people to think about people who cannot speak. So she used sign language for part of her speech.

Presenters Richard Gere, Susan Sarandon, and Tim Robbins have all spoken against China. They wanted Tibet to be a free country.

The big movie

In some years, a number of movies do well at the Oscars. But sometimes one movie is the big winner. In 1988, it was Bertolucci's movie about China, *The Last Emperor*. The movie had nine nominations. It won all of them.

One of the most successful movies in Oscar history is the Best Picture in 1960, *Ben-Hur*. The star of the movie was Charlton Heston. The movie was very long—over three and a half hours. It was also very expensive—the movie cost $15 million, a lot of money at that time. In fact, the studio was worried about the movie's success: it *had* to do well.

Ben-Hur was nominated for twelve Oscars. It won eleven of them. This was a lot, but in 1960 the Academy gave more awards. They gave different technical awards to color movies and to black-and-white movies. This only ended in 1967.

This exciting race was the most famous part of Ben-Hur.

King of the world!

Another big winner in Oscar history is also the most successful movie that was ever made. James Cameron's *Titanic* took a long time to make. It cost almost $200 million. Not everyone was sure about its success, but Cameron was not worried.

Soon everybody knew that the director was right. The movie was a great success all around the world. It earned over $1.6 billion!

The movie was nominated for fourteen awards in 1998. It won eleven. It was named the Best Picture. Cameron was named Best Director. But the movie's actors were not successful:

- Leonardo DiCaprio was not nominated and he did not go to the Oscars. Some people say that Cameron and DiCaprio were not friendly. DiCaprio says that this was not true.
- The movie's actresses did not have much more success. In *Titanic*, Kate Winslet played Rose when she was young. Another actress, Gloria Stuart, played the same person when she was old. Both actresses were nominated. Neither won.

AN OSCAR MEMORY ★ ★ ★ ★ ★ ★ ★ ★ ★ ★

In Cameron's speech, he held up the Oscar and repeated a famous line from the movie: "I'm king of the world!" He later joked, "Size does matter!"

★ ★ ★ ★ ★ ★ ★ ★ ★ ★ ★ ★ ★ ★ ★ ★ ★ ★

Titanic *was the most expensive movie ever.*

Everything about *Titanic* was big. It won its awards during the longest Oscar show ever!

The big and the small

In the same year a small British movie, *The Full Monty*, was nominated. It was a funny movie about a group of men who did not have jobs. They decided to take their clothes off on stage for money. The movie only cost three million dollars to make. But, it earned over two hundred million dollars. *The Full Monty* won one Oscar that year, for its music.

Actors *and* directors

A lot of actors decide to try directing. Some of them are successful, others are not. But in the 1990s, two big movie stars were very successful as directors.

Dances With Wolves was a special movie for actor Kevin Costner. The story was about an American soldier who meets American Indians. The movie's title was the name that the Indians gave to the soldier.

Six big movie studios said "no" to Costner and the movie idea. Finally, he went to a smaller company. During the meeting, Costner put on the soldier's clothes and rode a horse! The company offered six million dollars. The actor gave his own money to the movie, also. He was not paid until the movie was out in theaters.

Dances With Wolves was a big success. It was nominated for ten Oscars in 1991. It won seven. Kevin Costner proudly accepted awards for Best Picture and Best Director.

Since his big win in 1991, Costner has had some bad luck with movies. He acted in *Waterworld* and *The Postman*. Both movies were very expensive, but both lost a lot of money.

Another successful actor and director is Mel Gibson. His first movie as director was called *The Man Without a Face*. Gibson was also the star of the movie.

Then, Gibson wanted to make a very different kind of movie—one with lots of action. He was interested in the

William Wallace, ready to fight the English.

true story of William Wallace. Wallace fought the English over 700 years ago. He was fighting to free his country, Scotland. A lot of the movie's facts were wrong, but most people were not worried about that. The movie was a big success. It was nominated for nine Oscars in 1996. None of these were for the actors. Like Kevin Costner, Mel Gibson took home a Best Director and a Best Picture Oscar.

Steven Spielberg's long wait

Many people think that the Academy likes more "serious" movies. They point to Steven Spielberg. For a long time, the most famous and successful director in the world did not win an Oscar for Best Picture or Best Director.

- *Jaws* was a big success. It was nominated for Best Picture in 1975, but it did not win.
- Two years later, Spielberg had another big success. *Close Encounters of the Third Kind* was about aliens. Spielberg was nominated for Best Director. He did not win.
- In 1982, Spielberg was nominated for Best Director for *Raiders of the Lost Ark*, the first Indiana Jones movie. He lost again.
- The next year was the same story. People around the world loved Spielberg's next movie about an alien, *E.T.—The Extra Terrestrial*. Again, he was nominated for Best Director. Again, he lost.

So what was the problem? Were Spielberg's movies *too* popular? Weren't they serious enough? The director's next movie was very serious. He made a movie of Alice Walker's book *The Color Purple*. Whoopi Goldberg and Oprah Winfrey were in it.

This movie got eleven nominations in 1986. Spielberg was not nominated for Best Director, but the movie was nominated for Best Picture. Was this Spielberg's year? No! The movie won nothing. His next serious movie, *Empire of the Sun*, was not nominated for Best Picture or Best Director in 1988.

Spielberg's early movies were exciting. But in the 1990s, he turned to the darkest subject of all. *Schindler's List* told a true story of Jewish people in Nazi Germany. Oskar Schindler, a German businessman, saved hundreds of people from the Nazis. In 1994, the movie won nine awards. And Spielberg finally won Best Director and Best Picture awards.

But Spielberg did not stop making exciting popular movies. In the same year, his *Jurassic Park* won one award.

Spielberg won his second Oscar for Best Director in 1999. It was another serious movie—*Saving Private Ryan*, about the Second World War. The movie lost to *Shakespeare in Love* for Best Picture.

The world loved E.T.

How to pick a winner

How can you guess which movies are going to win? It is not easy, but winners from the past can give you some ideas.

Don't laugh!
The Academy often likes movies that are about serious subjects. *Driving Miss Daisy* was about the history of race problems in the United States. *American Beauty* questioned modern life in the United States. Two movies about the Vietnam war—*The Deer Hunter* and *Platoon*—have won Best Picture. One thing is true for many Oscar winners: they are long. Only two Best Pictures have ever been under 100 minutes.

From the history books
A lot of Best Picture winners have been about famous people from history: *Gandhi, Braveheart, The Last Emperor, Lawrence of Arabia, Amadeus*. But not all of these true stories are very serious: the cowboy movie *Butch Cassidy and the Sundance Kid*, with Robert Redford and Paul Newman, had a lot of laughs and action.

A happy message
Sometimes the Academy chooses movies with a happy message. People feel good after seeing them. The British movie about Olympic runners, *Chariots of Fire*, was like this. In 1976, another "feel-good" sports movie won. It was *Rocky*, Sylvester Stallone's first movie about boxing. *Taxi Driver* lost to *Rocky*. Many people now think that *Taxi Driver* with Robert De Niro is one of the best movies of the 1970s. But it was not a "feel-good" movie.

But be careful!

- Not many comedies have won Best Picture Oscars. Many winners have funny parts, but they are not really comedies. The last winning comedy was probably Woody Allen's *Annie Hall*.
- Musical movies have not done well for a long time either. In the 1960s, four musicals won. But the day of the musical movie seems to be at an end.
- Horror movies have done badly at the Oscars. *The Exorcist* was nominated, but it did not win. *The Silence of the Lambs* is the closest. It scared a lot of people, but it was not exactly a horror movie.

Clint Eastwood in Unforgiven.

But, remember—there are a lot of different kinds of people in the Academy. It is very hard to guess the winner. Hollywood made many great cowboy movies, but none won Best Picture. Then, in 1992, Clint Eastwood directed *Unforgiven*, a movie about an old cowboy. It won the Oscar.

Who knows what will win next year?

"Oops! We made a mistake!"

Some very famous movies and actors did not win Oscars. Actors Richard Burton and Peter O'Toole were both nominated seven times. Neither of them ever won! Here are some other "famous losers":

Singing' in the Rain (1952) This movie, with Gene Kelly, has been a favorite for years. It did not win any Oscars.

Shane (1953) Many people think that this was one of the best cowboy movies ever.

Rebel Without a Cause (1955) This is the movie which made James Dean famous.

Some Like it Hot (1959) Marilyn Monroe, Jack Lemmon, and Tony Curtis starred in this movie. It only won an Oscar for its clothes. In the movie, Lemmon and Curtis had to dress as women.

Psycho (1960) This black-and-white movie was not even nominated. But many people thought that it was Alfred Hitchcock's best. It was about a small hotel with a dark, dark secret. After they saw this movie, some people were afraid of the shower for years!

Dr. Strangelove (1964) The world is destroyed at the end of Stanley Kubrick's dark movie about war. But the movie was very funny, too! It was nominated, but did not win.

A Clockwork Orange (1971) A gang of young criminals runs through a Britain of the future. After some young people copied parts of the movie, director Stanley Kubrick refused to show the movie in Britain. People could only see it again after Kubrick died.

The biggest mistake?

Maybe the most famous "loser" in the Oscars was Orson Welles's movie *Citizen Kane*. The movie told the life story of a rich newspaper owner. Welles wrote and directed the movie, and he also acted in it. The movie's style was different and exciting.

Today, this movie is number one in many lists of the best movies ever. In 1941, Welles was nominated for many Oscars. But he won only one—for writing the movie. The movie was not named Best Picture. In some people's opinion, the awards that night "destroyed" Orson Welles.

Orson Welles in Citizen Kane.

The sound of music

The Oscars are not just for actors and actresses. Many other big stars have also won Oscars. These music stars have won Oscars for songs in movies:

- Lionel Ritchie for the song "Say You, Say Me" from *White Nights*.
- Carly Simon for "Let the River Run" from *Working Girl*.
- Prince for "Purple Rain" from the movie of the same name.
- Bruce Springsteen for "Streets of Philadelphia" from *Philadelphia*.
- Elton John for "Can You Feel the Love Tonight?" from *The Lion King*.

Many other big stars have been nominated: Pete Townshend, Dolly Parton, Phil Collins, Jon Bon Jovi, Bryan Adams, and Janet Jackson. Sometimes music stars sing during the show. Celine Dion sang "My Heart Will Go On" when *Titanic* was nominated. Bruce Springsteen sang when *Philadelphia* was nominated. Madonna sang at the Oscars in 1990. Her song "I Always get My Man," from *Dick Tracy*, won an award.

Which movies did these Oscar-winning songs come from? Choose from the list of movies.

1 "Talk to the Animals"	a *Doctor Doolittle*
2 "When You Wish Upon a Star"	b *The Wizard of Oz*
3 "Over the Rainbow"	c *Top Gun*
4 "Up Where We Belong"	d *An Officer and a Gentleman*
5 "Take My Breath Away"	e *Dirty Dancing*
6 "I've Had The Time of My Life"	f *Pinocchio*

You can find the answers on page 41.

Party, party, party!

For many years, there have been parties after the Oscars. Now there are parties before and after the Oscar show.

The British Academy of Film and Television Arts (BAFTA) in Los Angeles has a tea party on the day before the Oscars. The movie studio Miramax has a party on the night before the Oscars. At the party, actors read out lines from different movies.

The biggest party is after the Oscar show. Around 1,600 people go to it. Some people think that this is the most expensive party in the country. It usually costs one million dollars.

But there are lots of other parties in LA that night. Elton John usually has a party. Money from the party goes to help people with AIDS.*

How can you get into these parties? There is one ticket that will always get you in. His name is Oscar!

AN OSCAR MEMORY ★ ★ ★ ★ ★ ★ ★ ★ ★

There are big parties in New York on Oscar night, too. And in 1997, the people of Fargo, North Dakota had a party for everybody in town. The movie *Fargo* won two Oscars that year!

★ ★ ★ ★ ★ ★ ★ ★ ★ ★ ★ ★ ★ ★ ★ ★ ★

---

*AIDS: a terrible illness that kills many people every year.

What now, Oscar?

What do winners do with their Oscars after they have won? Most people put them in a safe place, of course. Many winners put their Oscars in a place where other people can see them, too. But some Oscars have had a strange time:

- Actor Clark Gable's Oscar was sold for over half a million dollars. Nobody knew who bought it. But it was given to the Academy as a gift. Some people think that Steven Spielberg was the secret buyer.

- Spencer Tracy starred in a movie called *Boys Town*. It was about a home where children without parents lived. After he won the Oscar, Tracy gave it to the real Boys Town.

- When actress Vivien Leigh was sick in the hospital, thieves came into her house. They stole an Oscar.

- Actor Ernest Borgnine's Oscar was lost in a house fire. The Academy gave him a new one.

- During the Second World War, the Oscars were not made of gold. New Oscars were easy to break. One winner broke his award by accident. He knocked its head off! The Academy gave him a new Oscar, too.

- Actor Jimmy Stewart won an Oscar for *The Philadelphia Story*. He put it in his father's store window.

- Some winners have sold their Oscars. One actor sold his award to pay for his wife's hospital bills. A writer sold his because he needed money. The Academy does not want winners to sell their Oscars. They have said that they will buy them back . . . for one dollar!

★ Where's Oscar? ★

In one year, the awards were lost before Oscar night! A poor man found them in the trash. He was a special guest at the Oscar show that year.

The police soon discovered the full story. Two van drivers stole the Oscars. When the story was on the news, they became scared. They kept two Oscars, and threw the others away.

"What's this? My lucky day?"

★   ★   ★   ★   ★   ★   ★   ★   ★

"What will I wear?"

When they are nominated, actors and actresses must make decisions about their clothes. It is not easy. They have six weeks to find the perfect clothes for the Oscars. The world will see them. Stars soon know if they have made a mistake. One actress says, "If you have a bad dress on, the red carpet outside the theater seems like . . . miles." If the clothes are right, everybody will want the same "look." But if the clothes are wrong, people will talk about them for years!

After the Oscars, some magazines and TV shows print lists of the best clothes. They also print lists of the worst! One year, singer Celine Dion put her coat on the wrong way. She says that it was a joke. But she was on a list of worst Oscar clothes the next day. Photos of her on Oscar night were in magazines for months.

Cher

Some stars are not worried about this. Cher is happy to be in the list of bad dressers. At one show she joked, "I dressed like an adult this year. I'm sorry. I'll never do it again!"

Oscar clothes are important, but stars do not *pay* for them. Almost every star wears clothes by a famous designer. Designers make the clothes in secret. Nobody sees them until Oscar night. Why do designers give stars these free clothes? They don't! Nothing is really free in Hollywood! Designers know that the world is watching. They want to show their clothes to the world. Stars usually thank the designers by name in interviews before the show. Many interviewers even ask, *"Who are you wearing?"* In fact, often stars wear the clothes for just the day of the Oscars. Then they give them back!

Some clothes companies watch the Oscars very carefully. They choose the best clothes and immediately copy them. Sometimes the clothes are ready to buy the next day. Not all Oscar clothes are easy to copy. In 1994, designer Lizzy Gardiner had a very strange dress. It was made out of American Express cards!

AN OSCAR MEMORY ★ ★ ★ ★ ★ ★ ★ ★ ★

One year, when the lights were on her, you could see through Barbra Streisand's clothes.

★ ★ ★ ★ ★ ★ ★ ★ ★ ★ ★ ★ ★ ★ ★ ★ ★ ★

Actress Sharon Stone chose her clothes one year. She wore a black skirt and a white shirt. The clothes were not by an expensive designer. They were from a clothes store that you can find in most towns and cities. Everybody thought she looked beautiful.

Often the right clothes are not enough. Stars want to wear the right jewelry, too. Like the clothes, stars wear the jewelry for one day and then they give it back.

This began in 1943. A man called Harry Winston had a jewelry store in Los Angeles. He gave some jewelry to an actress for Oscar night only. Winston became famous. There was even a line about him in a Marilyn Monroe song. The line said, "Talk to me, Harry Winston—Tell me all about it."

Now, when they have received a nomination, big stars often get a letter from the House of Harry Winston. They can go to one of the stores in New York, Beverly Hills, Paris, Geneva, or Tokyo and pick jewelry for the big night. One day, they had actresses Goldie Hawn and Mira Sorvino and television presenter Daisy Fuentes in the Beverly Hills store. Then Mel Gibson walked in, too!

Every year now the House of Harry Winston gives out two hundred million dollars in jewelry for the Oscars. And it all comes back to the store the next day!

AN OSCAR MEMORY ★ ★ ★ ★ ★ ★ ★ ★ ★

Claudia Schiffer called to get jewelry on the day of the show. They said no—she was too late. She was not late the next year.

★ ★ ★ ★ ★ ★ ★ ★ ★ ★ ★ ★ ★ ★ ★ ★ ★ ★

Other awards

The Oscars are the most important awards in movies. But there are other important awards:

- The Critics Choice Awards are early in the year. Maybe Academy voters think about these awards when they are making nominations for Oscars?
- Now the British Academy of Film and Television Awards (BAFTAs) are before the Oscars.
- The Golden Globe Awards are probably the biggest other awards. Foreign critics vote for these.

People at the Academy watch the Golden Globe Awards closely. The winners of these awards often win at the Oscars later. But in 1999, *The Cider House Rules* did badly at the Golden Globes. Then it got seven Oscar nominations and two Oscars!

Actor and director Warren Beatty has said, "The Golden Globes are fun. The Oscars are business." A lot of people probably do not agree with this. In their opinion, the Oscars are business AND fun!

Answers from page 1:
1 a   2 b   3 b   4 c   5 b   6 c   7 a   8 b
How many did you get right?
6–8 You are a star! You win an Oscar!
4–5 You are nominated for an Oscar.
0–3 You need this book!

Answers from page 34:
1a   2 f   3 b   4 d   5 c   6 e

ACTIVITIES

Pages 1–11

Before you read

1 Answer the questions. Find the words in *italics* in your dictionary. They are all in this book.

    a Is an *academy* one person or many people?

    b Do you buy or win an *award*?

    c Do you find *carpet* on the floor or the ceiling?

    d Does *comedy* make you laugh or cry?

    e Where do people in *wheelchairs* sit in movie theaters in your country?

2 Answer the questions with the words on the right. Who:

    a decides to make and sell   a *presenter*

        a movie?   a *supporting actor*

    b makes a movie?   a *studio*

    c *nominate* movies for   the *director*

        Academy awards (Oscars)?   *members* of the Academy

    d plays a small part in a movie?

    e hands an award to the winner?

3 What do you know about the Oscars? Try the questions on page 1.

After you read

4 Why:

    a are Oscars important for studios?

    b was the Academy started?

    c did the Academy decide that TV was not the enemy?

    d did the Academy stop gifts from studios to Academy members?

5 Describe how Oscar winners are chosen.

6 Who would you like to meet at an Oscar show? Why?

Pages 12–29

Before you read

7 What happens at an Oscar awards show?

8 Discuss these questions. Find the words in *italics* in your dictionary.

    a How many movies can you name with *aliens* in them?

    b How many people or companies can you name who *design* clothes?

    c Who would you like to *host* the Oscars? Why?

    d In your opinion, which new movie should receive a *technical* award?

    e Has anyone ever *clapped* for you? Why?

After you read

9 Why:

    a did Billy Crystal ride a horse onto the stage?

    b did Sharon Stone ask people to close their eyes?

    c did David Niven say, "This is the only laugh he will ever get"?

    d did Louise Fletcher say, "I've loved being hated by you"?

    e does the band sometimes play while people on stage are talking?

    f doesn't Woody Allen go to the Oscar awards show?

    g did James Cameron say, "I'm king of the world!"?

10 Discuss these questions.

    a In your opinion, why are Hollywood movies so popular around the world?

    b What movie from your country should win an Oscar?

Pages 30–41

Before you read

11 What kinds of movies win awards, do you think?

12 Answer the questions. Find the words in *italics* in your dictionary.

    a If you make a *choice* between two things, what do you do?

    b If you are a television *critic*, what do you write about?

    c When you watch a *horror* movie, how do you feel?

    d When you wear a lot of *jewelry*, where are you going?

After you read

13 Discuss the movies on pages 32–33. How many have you seen? What were they about? Do you think they were great movies? Why (not)?

Writing

14 You have won an Oscar. Write your speech.

15 You write for a newspaper. Write "The Story Behind the Oscars."

16 What are your nominations for this year's Best Picture, Best Actor, and Best Actress? Why?

17 You want to start new movie awards. What awards would you like to give? Why?

3 1221 08472 7762

Answers for the Activities in this book are available from your local office or alternatively write to: Penguin Readers Marketing Department, Pearson Education, Edinburgh Gate, Harlow, Essex CM20 2JE.